Making MASKS

Written and Illustrated by
Renée Schwarz

KIDS CAN PRESS

For Pippa, who always helps;
for Sophie, who is great at making faces;
and for Alex, who finds cool stuff for me

Text and illustrations © 2002 Renée Schwarz

KIDS CAN DO IT and the 🎨 logo are trademarks of Kids Can Press Ltd.

Kids Can Press acknowledges the support of the Government of Canada, through the BPIDP, for our publishing activity.

Published in Canada by
Kids Can Press Ltd.
29 Birch Avenue
Toronto, ON M4V 1E2

Published in the U.S. by
Kids Can Press Ltd.
2250 Military Road
Tonawanda, NY 14150

www.kidscanpress.com

Edited by Maggie MacDonald   Designed by Karen Powers
Photography by Frank Baldassarra
Printed and bound in Singapore

The hardcover edition of this book is smyth sewn casebound.
The paperback edition of this book is limp sewn with a drawn-on cover.

CM 02 0 9 8 7 6 5 4 3 2
CM PA 02 0 9 8 7 6 5 4 3 2 1

National Library of Canada Cataloguing in Publication Data

Schwarz, Renée
Making masks

(Kids can do it)

ISBN 1-55074-929-3 (bound)   ISBN 1-55074-931-5 (pbk.)

1. Mask making — Juvenile literature. 2. Paper work — Juvenile literature. I. Title. II. Series.

TT898.S36 2002   j646.4'78   C2001-903108-4

Kids Can Press is a *corus*™ Entertainment company

Contents

Introduction

Masks are fun! They have been used for celebrations and ceremonies, dances and plays for thousands of years.

The masks in this book are made from everyday materials and are easy to make. They feel comfortable and allow you to see well. This book shows you how to create many unique masks, but remember, for each type of mask, there are other characters just waiting for you to imagine and make. When you're finished wearing the mask, hang it on your wall as a decoration.

For parties, plays or dressing up, masks are great! Hidden behind a mask, you can become anyone or anything. So, for serious acting or simply for silly fun, make a mask.

MATERIALS

Many of the supplies you need can be found around the house and in your pencil case. Others are available at craft or hardware stores. Refer to these pages when gathering your materials.

Cutting tools

You will need scissors, and sometimes an X-Acto or craft knife, to cut out shapes. Always ask an adult to help you with an X-Acto knife, and protect your work surface with a piece of cardboard. For cutting wire or pipe cleaners, you will need wire cutters.

Hole punch

A hole punch makes nice round holes for tying the elastic to the sides of your mask. And you can use the dots or holes for decoration.

Glue and tape

For joining pieces together, you need white glue, a glue stick, a stapler and masking tape. A hot glue gun can be used, but only with an adult's help. Sometimes you will need a stronger tape, such as duct tape. Colored electrical tape is great for decorating — it both tapes and adds color. Clothespins and elastic bands come in handy for clamping while the glue dries.

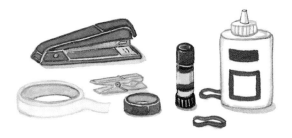

Cardboard

Quite a few of the masks are made with cardboard. Often, white or colored cardboard such as bristol board is used. It is available at art and craft stores. The thicker three-ply bristol board is better because it is stiffer. Corrugated cardboard, which brown boxes are made from, is also used. Because corrugated cardboard is much thicker, it makes the masks more three-dimensional. Lightweight cardboard, which is also available at art and craft stores, is good for decorating. When it is cut into strips, you can curl it with scissors.

Plastic screening

Plastic screening is available at hardware stores. It cuts easily, it's soft and you can see through it, so it is great to use for hiding your eyes.

Elastic and ribbon

To hold your mask in place, use either braided elastic, available at fabric stores, or ribbon. The elastic is better because it stretches and holds the mask tightly but comfortably on your face.

Decorations

Here are a few examples of things you can decorate your masks with: feathers, felt, pipe cleaners, sequins, stickers, ribbons and hardware odds and ends. You can also use pencils and markers for drawing and decorating.

Papier-mâché supplies

Newspaper and goo made from flour and water are all you need (see the recipe for papier-mâché goo on page 7).

Tips and techniques

MAKING EYE OPENINGS

When you wear a mask, your vision is always a bit blocked. It is important to make the eye openings quite large, especially at the sides, so that you can see well. To mark the eye openings, hold the mask in front of your face, then make a dot with a pencil as if you were trying to touch your eye.

Never poke a hole through the mask, either with a pencil or scissors, while holding it in front of your face!

Cut out the openings and try on the mask. Adjust if necessary.

Making a paper pattern with basic eye openings that fit you well is a good idea. You can use this pattern for most of your masks. Just change the eye shape a bit.

WEARING THE MASK

Your mask should fit snugly. Punch a hole at each side of the mask just above ear level. Push each end of a 50 cm (20 in.) elastic through a hole. Tie a knot at each end. Try on the mask and jump around. If necessary, tighten the elastic or add a second one higher up.

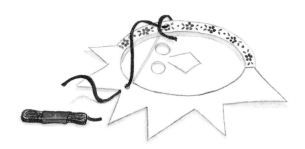

When wearing a mask, take your time and move about carefully. Look around you and don't run.

PAINTING TIPS

Refer to this section when you are ready to paint.

● Before starting, cover your work surface with a plastic bag.

● You will need: paint, a few different-sized paintbrushes, plastic lids for palettes and a glass jar for water.

- Acrylic paint works best because it dries quickly, it won't flake off, and the colors are bright.

- It is best to paint your mask first with a coat of white primer paint or gesso. Allow to dry.

- Allow paint to dry between colors.

- Use big, bold designs, so they can be seen from far away.

- You can also use tissue paper to paint your mask. See step 11 on page 28 for instructions.

- Don't let paint dry on your brush.

PAPIER-MÂCHÉ GOO

In a saucepan, mix together 500 ml (2 c.) water and 125 ml (½ c.) white flour. With help from an adult, cook the mixture on medium heat, stirring constantly, until thick. Pour the goo into a plastic container and let cool a few minutes before using. Refrigerate leftover goo.

PAPIER-MÂCHÉ TECHNIQUE

1. Before starting, cover your work surface with a plastic bag.

2. Tear newspaper into strips, 2.5 cm x 15 cm (1 in. x 6 in.).

3. Coat each strip with a thin layer of goo.

4. Cover your mask completely with one layer of strips, then add another layer, placing the strips in the opposite direction.

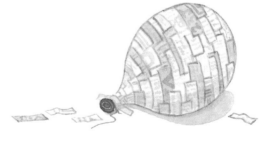

5. After applying five layers of papier-mâché, let your piece dry for at least one day.

Crazy cat

You can make a dog or mouse for the other hand!

YOU WILL NEED

- white or colored cardboard, 30 cm x 45 cm (12 in. x 18 in.)
- a length of wood, 30 cm x 1 cm (12 in. x ½ in.), or a wooden ruler
- painting supplies (page 6)
- 2 green pipe cleaners
- a pencil, scissors, a ruler, glue, markers, tape

1 Draw the head on the cardboard. Cut it out.

2 Draw on the eyes and cut them out. Check that you can see well through the mask. Adjust if necessary.

3 Glue the top 10 cm (4 in.) of the stick to the back of the mask and hold it with tape. Let dry.

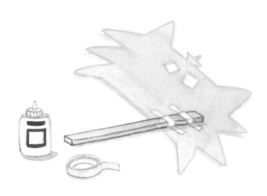

4 Paint the mask (see the painting tips on page 6) or decorate it with markers.

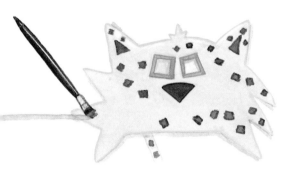

5 With the tip of your scissors, carefully poke two small holes on each side of the nose.

6 From the back, poke the ends of a pipe cleaner through the holes on either side of the nose. Repeat with the other pipe cleaner for the other two holes. Secure with tape.

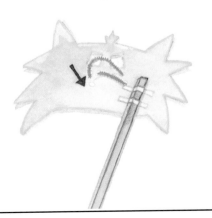

OTHER IDEAS

And now for your other hand!

Dog

Mouse

Ugly bugly bug

Great for bugging friends. Wear it with a swim cap and a striped T-shirt.

YOU WILL NEED

- a Styrofoam pipe insulation tube, 90 cm (1 yd.) long with a 1 cm (½ in.) inside diameter
- colored electrical tape
- 12 pipe cleaners: 6 black, 2 green, 2 red, 2 yellow
- a ruler, scissors

1 Cut the Styrofoam tube in half lengthwise so that you have two long strips. Mark the middle of one of the strips with a piece of tape.

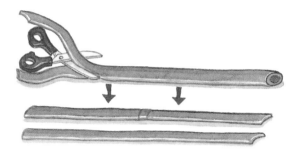

2 Roll up one end of this strip so that it forms a circle on one side of the center mark. Hold it in place with tape. Do the same with the other end. You now have an eyeglass shape.

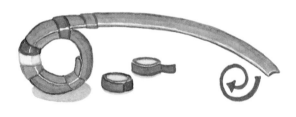

3 Cut the other Styrofoam strip to the length you want the stinger to be.

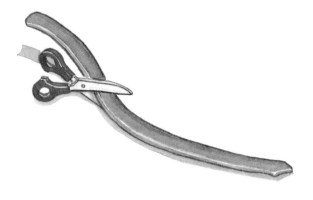

4 Decorate the eyeglasses and the stinger with bands of colored tape.

5 Make striped pipe cleaners by twisting two different-colored pipe cleaners together.

6 Poke two striped pipe cleaners through the stinger about 2.5 cm (1 in.) from the top. Make little blobs at the ends so that the pipe cleaners don't slip through. Then poke the pipe cleaners through the top of the mask, at the center. Twist them together once to hold the stinger in place.

7 Tape the glasses together just below the stinger.

8 Poke two striped pipe cleaners through the top of the mask for another set of antennae. Make little blobs at the ends, then shape the antennae.

9 Poke the remaining striped pipe cleaners through the sides of the mask. Twist the ends together to hold the mask on your face.

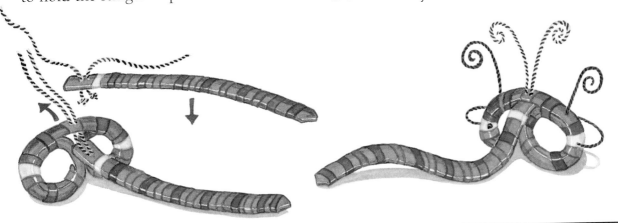

Moon and Sun

A heavenly combination!

YOU WILL NEED

- a large paper plate
- white cardboard
- clothespins
- painting supplies (page 6)
- paper: gold, silver
- 2 ribbons, each 45 cm (18 in.) long
- a pencil, a ruler, scissors, glue, tape, a hole punch

1 Draw the eyes on the paper plate about 8 cm (3 in.) from the top. They should be at least 3 cm (1¼ in.) in diameter. Cut them out.

2 Draw a diamond-shaped nose on the plate. The diamond should be about 6 cm (2¼ in.) long and start at mid-eye level. Cut it out, leaving the top 1 cm (½ in.) attached.

3 Draw a slightly larger nose on the white cardboard and cut it out. It should be about 1 cm (½ in.) longer at the top. Glue the cardboard nose to the paper plate nose. Be careful not to glue it to the rest of the plate. Let the glue dry.

4 To make the sun's rays, place the plate onto the cardboard and trace around half of it. Remove the plate and add an extra 2 cm (3/4 in.) to the inside of the circle, then draw the rays around the outside. Cut out and glue to the back of the plate. Clamp with clothespins until dry. Secure with tape on the back.

6 Draw a moon shape on silver paper and sun shape on gold paper. Trace on the eye openings. Cut out the shapes and glue them to the mask.

7 To decorate, punch holes out of the gold and silver paper, and cut out stripes, stars and suns. Glue them to the mask.

5 Paint the mask yellow, gold and blue (see the painting tips on page 6).

8 Punch holes at each side of the mask, just above ear level. Tie on ribbons.

Jolly jester

*Once you've made this mask,
you just need to learn how to juggle!*

YOU WILL NEED

- plastic sunglasses
- white cardboard
- painting supplies (page 6)
- 8 small gold bells
- 8 metallic pipe cleaners:
  4 blue, 2 red, 2 gold
- curled ribbons: 3 gold, 2 red
- star stickers or dots: red, gold
- elastic, 45 cm (18 in.)
- a pencil, a ruler, scissors, glue,
  a hole punch

1 Trace the outline of the sunglass frame on the cardboard, about 10 cm (4 in.) from the bottom.

2 Draw the hat and nose around the outline. The hat should extend 2.5 cm (1 in.) past the sides of the glasses and 1 cm (½ in.) below the top. Cut out the shape.

3 Place the shape on another piece of cardboard and trace around. Cut it out, then glue the two pieces together and let dry.

4 Punch holes near the tips of the hat and at the bottom corners. Also punch out the openings for the glasses' arms, leaving a 1 cm (½ in.) edge on the inside. The opening should be two or three holes long so that the arms fit in tightly. Insert the glasses and try on the mask.

5 Remove the glasses and paint the front and back of the mask (see the painting tips on page 6). Let dry.

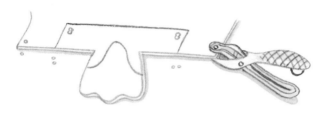

6 Thread a bell onto the end of each pipe cleaner. Wind the pipe cleaners around a pencil to curl them. Attach the pipe cleaners as shown to the holes in the hat and tie on the ribbons.

7 Decorate the hat with star stickers or dots.

8 Insert the glasses and tie an elastic to the ends of the arms to hold the mask in place. Start juggling!

OTHER IDEAS

How about a juggling chicken? Careful with the eggs.

Lordly lion

Have a roaring good time when you prowl around as king of the beasts.

YOU WILL NEED

- a large plate, about 25 cm (10 in.) in diameter
- cardboard
- felt: yellow, red, orange, white, blue, brown
- elastic, 50 cm (20 in.)
- raffia* or wool: beige, brown, yellow, orange, red
- a pencil, scissors, a ruler, glue, a hole punch

* Raffia is made of plant fiber. It comes in lots of neat colors.

1 Place the large plate on the cardboard and trace around it. Cut out the circle.

2 Draw the eyes on the cardboard mask about 9 cm (3½ in.) from the top. Also draw a triangular nose opening. Cut out the eyes and along three sides of the nose, leaving the top 1 cm (½ in.) attached.

3 Place the cardboard mask onto a piece of yellow felt. Trace around the outside and around the eye and nose openings. Cut out, leaving the top of the nose attached. Glue the felt to the cardboard and let dry.

4 Ask an adult to punch holes all around the mask, about 1 cm (½ in.) from the edge and at least 1 cm (½ in.) apart.

5 Tie elastic to a hole on each side of the mask, just above your ears. Check that you can see well through the mask. Adjust if necessary.

6 Cut the raffia into 33 cm (13 in.) lengths. Fold a few strands in half, then poke them through a hole. Pull the ends through the loop and gently pull the knot tight. Continue knotting this way all the way around.

7 Cut out four felt ears. Glue together in pairs and let dry. Cut a 2 cm (¾ in.) slit in the center of each ear. Overlap the edges and glue together. Let glue dry. Glue the ears to the head.

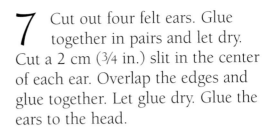

8 Cut out felt decorations: red mouth, white teeth, brown nose and ear insides, eye whites, blue stars, orange "crow's-foot" wrinkles, and red eyebrows. Glue them to the mask. Let dry.

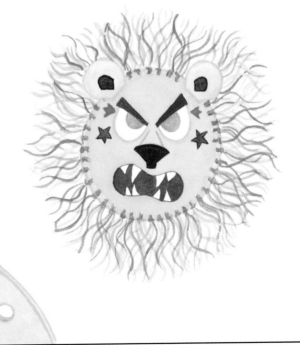

Ferocious fish

*You won't need to fish for compliments
with this on your head!*

YOU WILL NEED

- a tall, narrow box that fits over your
head, 35 cm x 29 cm x 23 cm
(14 in. x 11½ in. x 9 in.)
- white cardboard
- corrugated cardboard
- a brown paper bag
- newspaper
- painting supplies (page 6)
- plastic screening
- scissors, a pencil, a ruler, glue,
an X-Acto or craft knife, tape

1 Remove all tape and stickers from
the box. Glue the bottom flaps
closed if necessary. Cut off the top flaps.

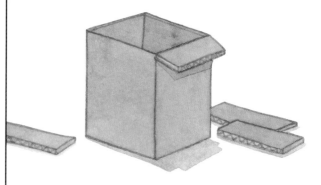

2 Place the box over your head so
that your nose touches it. Mark
where your shoulders are. Remove the
box and cut out the shoulder rests.
Round off the front and back of the box.

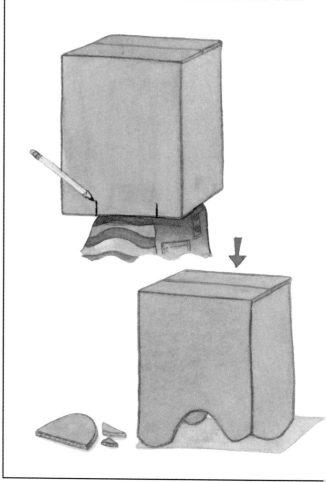

3 Draw the mouth on the front of the box and around the sides. The opening should be about 8 cm (3 in.) wide and 9 cm (3½ in.) from the top of the box. Cut out the mouth. Try on the box and check that you can see well. Adjust if necessary.

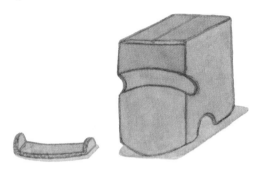

4 Draw the tail and fins (one dorsal and two side fins) on the white cardboard and cut them out. Round off the points so they won't poke anyone.

5 Place the shapes on another piece of white cardboard, trace around them and cut them out. Glue the pieces together, leaving a 2.5 cm (1 in.) strip unglued along the straight ends. Let dry.

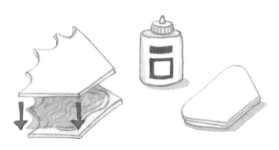

6 Ask an adult to cut slits with an X-Acto knife in the top, the sides and the back of the box, where you want the tail and the fins to be. Slip the straight ends through the slits.

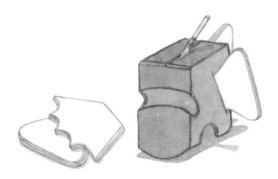

7 Fold out the unglued parts of the tail and fins and glue them to the inside of the box.

8 Cut two large round eyes out of corrugated cardboard. Glue them to the front of the box so that they stick out over the top. Let dry.

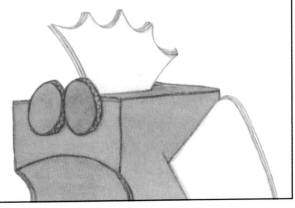

Instructions continue on the next page ☞

9 Stuff the paper bag with crumpled newspaper and tape it closed. Place it inside the box at the back and try on the mask. Your head should fit into the mask snugly. Adjust if necessary. Glue the bag in place.

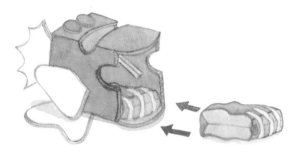

10 Apply gesso and paint the fish (see the painting tips on page 6). Fish are all sorts of wild colors and patterns, so you can go crazy.

11 Cut out lots of white cardboard teeth and glue them to the inside of the mouth.

12 Tape one or two layers of plastic screening to the inside of the mouth to hide your eyes.

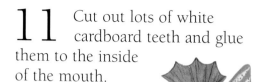

OTHER IDEAS

🎭 For a totally different look, make a robot head. Paint the box metallic gray and glue on hardware odds and ends.

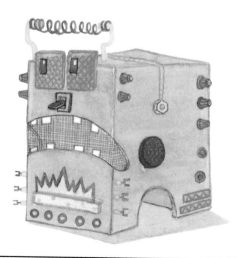

Fearless falcon

In ancient Egypt, a falcon mask would be worn in special ceremonies.

YOU WILL NEED

- felt: black, gray, white, yellow
- a gray baseball cap • sequins
- a Styrofoam ball, 10 cm (4 in.) in diameter
- 4 toothpicks
- painting supplies (page 6)
- feathers: black, white
- a strip of stiff cardboard, 2.5 cm x 15 cm (1 in. x 6 in.)
- black tulle fabric, 25 x 35 cm (10 in. x 14 in.)
- scissors, glue, a ruler, hot glue and a glue gun, an X-Acto or craft knife

1 Cut two long wings from the black felt.

2 Glue the wings to a slightly larger piece of gray felt so that one is the mirror image of the other. Let dry, then trim all around, leaving a 0.5 cm (¼ in.) border. Glue the wings gray side down to a piece of white felt. Let dry and trim around as before.

3 Glue the wings to the sides of the cap and let them dry.

Instructions continue on the next page ☞

4 From the yellow and black felt, cut out four 2.5 cm (1 in.) wide strips of different lengths, 25 cm to 55 cm (10 in. to 22 in.). Cut bumps approximately the width of your thumb along one edge of each strip.

5 With an adult's help, hot glue sequins to the bumps, then glue the strips, alternating the colors, to the front of the cap. Let dry.

6 Ask an adult to use an X-Acto knife to cut 2.5 cm (1 in.) off the bottom of the Styrofoam ball and 1 cm (½ in.) off one side. Gently shape the flattened bottom of the ball by pressing with your thumb, so that it fits the curve of the cap's visor.

7 Cut a beak about 3.5 cm x 5 cm (1½ in. x 2 in.) from the Styrofoam scrap.

8 Attach the beak near the top of the Styrofoam ball head with the toothpicks.

9 Paint the head, but not the bottom, with gesso. Let dry. Apply a second coat of gesso. Let dry, then paint with acrylic paints (see the painting tips on page 6).

10 Glue black feathers to the visor. Let dry.

11 Glue the head onto the visor, over the feathers. Hold the head in place for a few minutes while the glue sets. Let dry.

12 Glue three long tail feathers to the end 4 cm (1½ in.) of the cardboard strip. Let dry. Fold as shown and glue to the inside of the cap so that the feathers stick out at the back. Let dry.

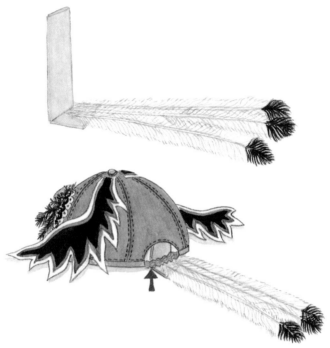

13 Glue a piece of black tulle fabric to the inside of the cap to hide your face. Let dry.

Lonely alien

A being from another world ...
the hardware store.

YOU WILL NEED

- a rubber bath mat with holes
- plastic screening,
  10 cm x 20 cm (4 in. x 8 in.)
- plastic-coated wire   • wire cutters
- pipe cleaners   • yellow nylon cord
- hardware odds and ends: wire nuts,
  2 orange self-adhesive reflectors,
  plastic screw anchors,
  spade terminals, a chain
- colored electrical tape
  and aluminized tape
- 2 pieces of elastic, each 50 cm (20 in.)
- a ruler, scissors, a pencil

1 Cut out a weird head shape about 47 cm long x 38 cm wide (18½ in. x 15 in.) from the mat.

2 Cut eye slits near the middle of the mask. Tape the plastic screening to the back to hide your eyes.

3 Weave some plastic-coated wire around the top half of the mask about 2.5 cm (1 in.) from the edge. The wire helps the mask keep its shape.

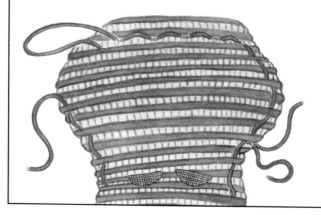

4 Wind the ends of the wire around a pencil to curl them. Screw wire nuts to the ends.

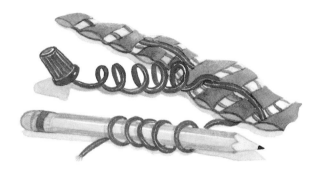

5 For the chin, lace the bottom of the mask together with pipe cleaners at the back.

6 For the hair, cut different lengths, 20 cm to 35 cm (8 in. to 14 in.), of yellow cord. Knot them around the top of the head, then untwist the ends to make them frizzy.

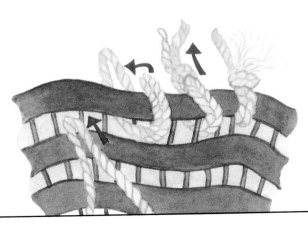

7 Peel off the backing and stick on the reflector eyes above the eye slits. Cut shapes from colored electrical and aluminized tape and decorate the mask.

8 Add other hardware. Poke plastic screw anchors through openings, and weave in other lengths of coated wire and curl the ends. Attach hardware with pipe cleaners.

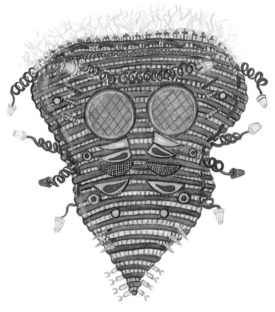

9 Tie two elastics at each side of the mask, one at ear level and one a bit higher, to hold the mask securely on your head.

Punk bird

This phoenix bird is ready to rock.

YOU WILL NEED

- a large empty bleach bottle, 3.6 L (1 gal.)
- elastic, 50 cm (20 in.)
- white or colored cardboard
- duct tape
- colored tissue paper
- acrylic gloss medium
  (or 50/50 mixture of white glue and water)
- a paintbrush and water jar
- an X-Acto or craft knife, a ruler, scissors, a pencil, a hole punch

1 Ask an adult to help you rinse the bleach bottle well and remove the label and glue.

2 Ask an adult to cut off the handle and the screw-thread top with an X-Acto knife.

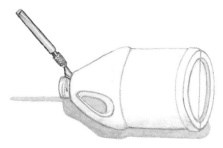

3 Cut a large opening with the scissors on the side where the handle was so that your head fits inside. The opening should be about 14 cm x 23 cm (5½ in. x 9 in.).

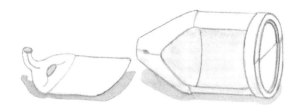

4 Put on the mask and mark where your eyes are — usually about 14 cm (5½ in.) from the top. Cut out the eyes.

5 Punch a hole on each side of the mask at ear level and tie on the elastic. Check that you can see well through the mask. Adjust the eyes if necessary.

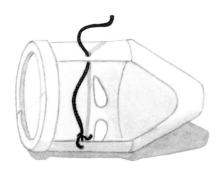

6 Cut out two beaks in the shape of a piece of pie from the white cardboard. Cut 1 cm (½ in.) deep slits along the top edges.

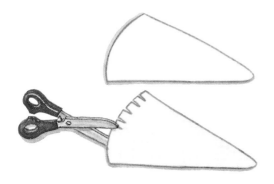

TIP *If you use colored cardboard for the beak and feathers, you won't have to cover them with tissue paper in step 11.*

7 Cut a curved slit in the bottle at least 1 cm (½ in.) below the eyes.

8 Slip the beaks through the slit from the inside of bottle until 1 cm (½ in.) remains inside. Fold the tabs back and tape them to the bottle.

9 Cut out 25 to 40 feather shapes of different lengths from the cardboard.

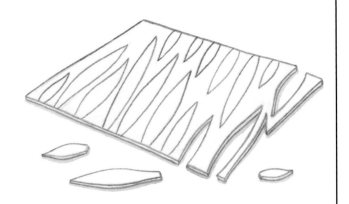

Instructions continue on the next page ☞

10 Cut small slits with scissors or an X-Acto knife in the top of the mask and around the sides. Insert the ends of the feathers, bend them and tape to the inside of the bottle.

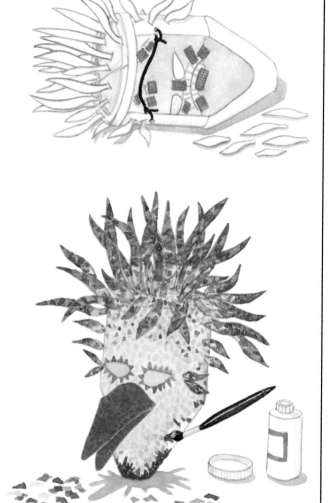

11 Paint the mask with tissue paper. Tear the tissue paper into small scraps, from 1 cm to 4 cm (½ in. to 1½ in.) long. Place a scrap of tissue paper on the bottle and paint over it with acrylic medium. Place another scrap beside it, so that the edges overlap, and coat with medium. Continue to cover the bottle, beak and feathers this way. Experiment by overlapping different color combinations and shapes, such as triangles, crescents and diamonds. Always soak your brush in water when you are not using it, because if the medium dries on your brush, it will not wash off.

12 Let dry ... then fly.

OTHER IDEAS

To make a weird witch, use beige and olive green tissue paper for skin and curled pipe cleaners for hair.

Dancing dragon

In ancient China, dragon masks were used in dances to ward off evil spirits.

YOU WILL NEED

- white cardboard
- corrugated cardboard
- duct tape
- colored tissue paper
- acrylic gloss medium (or 50/50 mixture of white glue and water)
- a paintbrush and water jar
- lightweight colored cardboard
- a ruler, a pencil, scissors, glue, a stapler

1 Draw the head on a sheet of white cardboard 50 cm x 60 cm (20 in. x 24 in.). The eyes should be about 15 cm (6 in.) from the top. Cut it out.

2 Place the head on another piece of white cardboard and trace around it. Cut it out and glue the two pieces together. Let dry.

3 Draw a nose on the white cardboard and cut it out. Trace it three times onto corrugated cardboard and cut out the shapes.

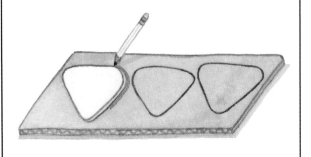

Instructions continue on the next page ☞

4 Glue the four nose pieces together with the white piece on top. Glue the nose to the head.

5 Draw two eyebrows on the white cardboard, adding an extra 1 cm (½ in.) along the bottom edge. Cut them out. Place them on another piece of white cardboard, trace and cut out. Glue together in pairs, leaving the extra 1 cm (½ in.) at the bottom unglued. Let dry, then fold out the unglued parts.

6 For the mouth, cut out two strips of white cardboard that are 4 cm x 27 cm (1½ in. x 11 in.) and two strips 4 cm x 21 cm (1½ in. x 8½ in.). Glue together in pairs, leaving a 2 cm (¾ in.) strip along a long edge unglued. Let dry, then fold out the unglued parts.

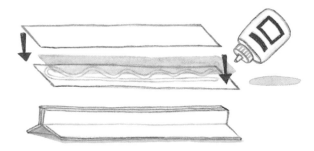

7 Cut slits about 1 cm (½ in.) apart along the unglued flaps of the eyebrows and mouth.

8 Spread glue on the bottom of the flaps, then glue the eyebrows and mouth to the head. Hold a few minutes while the glue sets.

9 Cut teeth (both triangles and rectangles) from white cardboard. Bend the ends, then glue them to the inside of the mouth. Let dry.

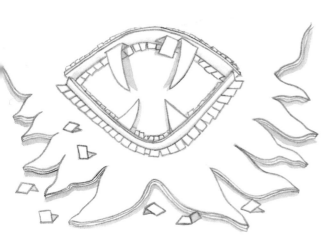

11 Paint the mask with tissue paper (see step 11 on page 28).

10 For the handles, cut out four 2 cm x 30 cm (3/4 in. x 12 in.) strips of white cardboard. Glue together in pairs. Let dry, then staple the ends to the back of the mask so that the middle forms a handle. Secure with tape.

12 From colored cardboard, cut 20 to 30 thin strips between 30 cm and 60 cm (12 in. and 24 in.) long. To curl the ends, hold the strip with your thumb against the edge of a pair of closed scissors, so that you do not cut yourself. Grasp the strip with your other hand, then carefully pull the scissors along without tearing the strip. Repeat if necessary. Tape the strips to the back of the chin and the forehead.

Knight and horse

A fighting pair, at your service.

YOU WILL NEED

- silver cardboard
- adhesive vinyl: red, blue, gold (or colored paper)
- a piece of plastic screening, 15 cm x 25 cm (6 in. x 10 in.)
- black cardboard
- a large paper cup • elastic bands
- 25 red pipe cleaners (cut in half)
- clothespins • curtain trim
- a ruler, a pencil, scissors, glue, tape, a stapler, a hole punch

KNIGHT

1 Cut the silver cardboard so that it is 27 cm (11 in.) wide and long enough to fit around your head with an overlap of about 3 cm (1¼ in.).

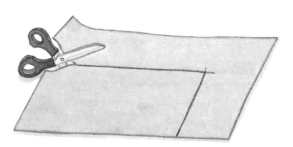

2 Draw the eye slit about 13 cm (5 in.) from the top. The slit should measure 2 cm x 18 cm (¾ in. x 7 in.).

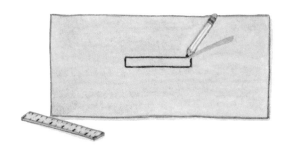

3 Draw an arrow-shaped nose so that it intersects the eye slit. Cut out the eye slits, cutting around the nose and leaving the top attached.

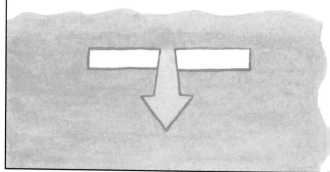

4 Decorate the mask using strips and shapes you have cut out of the adhesive vinyl, or glue on colored paper cutouts.

5 Tape the piece of plastic screening to the inside of the mask to hide your eyes.

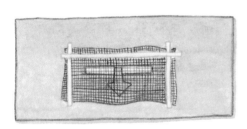

6 Make the mask into a cylinder by overlapping the ends and gluing them together. Staple or secure with tape on the inside. Let dry, then check that you can see well through the mask.

HORSE

1 Cut the black cardboard so that it is 23 cm (9 in.) wide and long enough to fit around your head with an overlap of about 3 cm (1¼ in.).

2 Place the paper cup on another piece of black cardboard and trace around the bottom. Add an extra 1 cm (½ in.) all around the circle and cut it out.

3 Make cuts all around, from the edge to the inner circle. Glue the circle to the bottom of the paper cup, folding the flaps down around the side. Hold with elastic bands until dry.

Instructions continue on the next page ☞

4 Cover the sides of the cup by rolling a piece of black cardboard around it. Trim off the extra, then glue it in place. Hold with elastics until dry. Gently squish the cup so that it is slightly oval.

5 Place the oval cup on the black cardboard mask about 2.5 cm (1 in.) from the bottom. Trace around the brim.

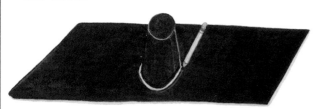

6 Cut out the oval 0.25 cm (⅛ in.) inside the line, so that the opening is a bit smaller.

7 Insert the cup through the hole from the back, up to the brim. It should fit tightly. Secure with tape on the inside.

8 Draw on the eyes. They should be centered slightly above the top of the muzzle. There should be a 1 cm (½ in.) space between the cup and the eyes. Cut out the eyes.

9 Repeat steps 4 and 6 on page 33.

10 For the mane, cut a strip of black cardboard 4 cm x 50 cm (1½ in. x 20 in.). Punch two alternating rows of holes about 2.5 cm (1 in.) apart, starting 6.5 cm (2½ in.) from one end. Using two half pipe cleaners, poke the ends through two adjacent holes, then twist them together. Continue the length of the cardboard.

11 Glue the mane to the inside of the mask at the front and down along the outside at the back. Clamp with clothespins until dry.

12 Draw ears on the black cardboard and cut them out. Cut a 6 cm (2¼ in.) slit in the center of each ear. Overlap the edges and staple in place.

13 Glue or staple the ears to the sides of the head, then decorate with adhesive vinyl or colored paper.

14 Glue curtain trim around the top of the head and along the muzzle. Let dry.

Dangerous dinosaur

Since no one knows what colors dinosaurs were, you can decide.

YOU WILL NEED

- olive green cardboard
- colored markers and pencils, a gold metallic pen
- lightweight cardboard: white, red, yellow, black, blue
- elastic, 50 cm (20 in.)
- clothespins
- a ruler, a pencil, scissors, glue, a hole punch

1 Draw the head on a 40 cm x 20 cm (16 in. x 8 in.) piece of green cardboard. The nose opening should be about 8 cm x 6 cm (3 in. x 2¼ in.). Cut out.

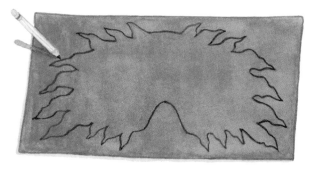

2 Draw on the eyes. They should be centered slightly above the top of the nose opening. Cut out and check that you can see well through the mask.

3 Cut out two snout pieces in the shape of a piece of pie about 20 cm x 9 cm (8 in. x 3½ in.).

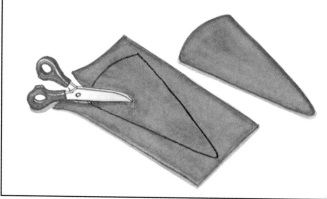

4 Decorate the face and one snout piece with scales using colored markers or pencils and a metallic pen.

5 From white cardboard, cut out lots of triangles for teeth. Bend the ends and glue them to the insides of the snout pieces, close to the edge.

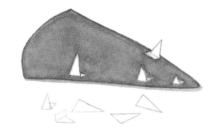

6 From the red cardboard, cut out two pieces that are slightly smaller than the snout. Glue them to the insides of the snout pieces.

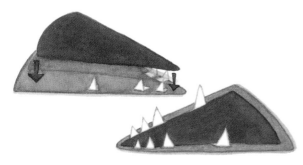

7 Cut eyebrows, eyeballs, tongue and crest from colored cardboard and glue them on the mask. Color lightly with pencils.

8 Cut slits that are 1 cm (½ in.) deep and 1 cm (½ in.) apart along the top of the snout pieces. Fold the flaps up.

9 Glue the flaps to the inside of the mask, around the nose opening. Clamp with clothespins until dry. Secure with tape if necessary.

10 Punch a hole at each side of the mask, at ear level, and tie on the elastic.

Grumpy green gargoyle

Gargoyles are ugly ... and proud of it!

YOU WILL NEED

- a big balloon • string
- papier-mâché supplies (page 5)
- corrugated cardboard
- aluminum foil, 90 cm (36 in.) long
- newspaper
- a french-fries box or a paper cup
- painting supplies (page 6)
- a neck warmer
- a ruler, tape, scissors, a pencil

1 Blow up the balloon so that it is much larger than your head, and knot it. Tie a string around the knot.

2 Tape the knotted end of the balloon to your work surface. Cover the balloon with five layers of papier-mâché (see page 7). Hang it from the string to dry for at least one day.

3 Cut a large hole in the side of the papier-mâché balloon, about 18 cm (7 in.) in diameter, so that your head fits inside. Remove the balloon.